Please direct inquiries t(

<u>More from the author</u>

Books:

- Hardcore Self Help: F**K Anxiety
- Hardcore Self Help: F**K Depression
- Does My Mom Have Dementia?

Online:

- The Hardcore Self Help Podcast
- Kick Anxiety's Ass online course – kickanxietycourse.com

If you would like to use any of these journal prompts for your own purposes, please do. Feel free to use them in your professional work or use them on social media. If you would like to tag me @duffthepsych or give me credit, I would greatly appreciate it.

Reviews are IMMENSELY helpful as well. If you found this book to be helpful, please consider leaving a review on Amazon.

Enjoy!

Introduction

You've probably heard about the benefits of journaling by now. God knows, I spend way too much time talking people's ears off about it. As a clinical psychologist, self-help author, and podcaster, I feel like I'm constantly telling people about how journaling is the best way to do "self-therapy". Uncomfortable feelings about the way your partner is acting? Journal about it. Confused about why you keep falling into the same patterns of resentment? Journal about it. Looking for ways to improve your productivity at work? Journal about it!

But I understand that it's often not as easy as saying, "Okay. Time to journal. 1, 2, 3, GO!" In fact, the blank page terrifies some people and really turns them off to the idea of journaling in the first place. I understand and I've got you covered.

This is a very powerful book. I spent the last few months locked away in an isolated cabin with nothing but my brain, a word processor, and just enough rations to get me through the harsh winter to bring you the best journal prompts to stimulate your creativity and provide a perfect platform for self-exploration. What you will find within this book are the fruits of that journey.

Okay that was a total lie. No cabin. No rations. I'm sitting in my airconditioned home office with an Aperol spritz as I write this intro. But the journal prompts really are good! I think there is something in here for everyone from deep explorations of your past to silly creativity activities to thought-provoking quotes.

I decided to keep this book bare-bones and randomized so that any time you want, you can flip to a page and find something to get your gears turning. Will you encounter a quirky exercise like thinking of alternate uses for a household object? Or will you be diving deep into your own psyche? Fate will decide.

While these prompts are designed for journaling, they can truly be used for a number of different purposes. If you are a podcast host, you could use these as interview questions to dive deeper with your guests. If you are therapist or coach, these could be great conversation prompts. If you suck at finding things to talk about on dates, bring this book along and get to know each other *really* well.

Before I stop blabbing and let you get to the journaling, I'd like to quickly give you a little structure. You absolutely don't have to use this format if you like simply starting with a blank page or have your own journaling method that you already prefer.
But I know some of you stress-cases out there need some extra direction, so here we go!

First, divide the page of your journal, notebook, etc. into three sections. One large section at the top and two small sections at the bottom with numbers 1-3. Like this:

1.	1.
2.	2.
3.	3.

Before tackling the top part, we are going to take a look at the two little sections at the bottom. On the left, I'm going to give you a task that may be very difficult… I want you to write down three things that you are currently proud of yourself for. Gasp! I know it is tough… that's the point. These can be small things like "I woke up on time today" or big things like "I finally set a boundary with my mom". Much like tracking gratitude, this will allow you to subtly change what your attention latches onto. It can gradually help you learn to give yourself credit and build self-efficacy.

On the other side, I want you do write down one to three of your most important "to do" items for the day. Similarly, these can be big or small tasks, but you MUST keep it to only one, two, or three items. You will obviously do more than three things in a day, but this forces you to think and prioritize. Think about the things that you could get done with your day that would leave you at least somewhat satisfied at the end of the day if you didn't do anything else. In the interest of being uncomfortable along with you, I'll fill in my own examples!

Proud Of	To Do
1. Got the podcast done last night even though I didn't feel like recording.	1. Finish intro and back matter for the new book.
2. Finished up the last of the journal prompts.	2. Figure out what continuing education courses I need to take for licensure renewal.
3. Allowed myself to sleep in since I've been feeling like hot garbage.	3. Spend some unplugged quality time with the kids.

After you are done with the bottom sections here, you move onto the blank part at the top. That is the actual journaling part. I know it can be scary to have a big empty section that you expect yourself to fill, but that's also the whole point of this book. Put a random prompt from the book at the top and start journaling!

Well… what are you waiting for? 1, 2, 3, journal!

500 Journal Prompts

1. What part of life has surprised you the most?

2. What is a reminder that you would like to tell yourself next time you are in a downward spiral?

3. How would your friends describe you? How do you feel about those descriptions?

4. Who is someone that significantly influenced the person you are now?

5. What are you looking forward to right now?

6. Think about the last time you cried. If those tears could talk, what would they have said?

7. Figure out where you do your best thinking and see how you can spend more time there.

8. What is the last song that you listened to on repeat? Why?

9. What are some movies or TV shows that make you feel encouraged or motivated?

10. What do you know about your genealogy? How do you feel about it?

11. React to the following quote from *The Fault in Our Stars* by John Green: "What a slut time is. She screws everybody."

12. Draw a small scribble on the page then use your imagination to turn that scribble into a full drawing.

13. Write an apology to yourself for a time you treated yourself poorly. Remember, a good apology should feature an acknowledgment of what happened, how it made the person feel, and how you will do better in the future.

14. If you could travel to anywhere in the world to live in another era, where and when would you go? If your gut instinct was that you'd rather stay where you are, why?

15. What is a made-up rule about your life that you are applying to yourself? How has this held you back and how might you change it?

16. Write about a time you can remember being blindsided by something someone told you.

17. How do you feel toward other people that you know have anxiety?

18. What is a positive habit that you would really like to cultivate? Why and how could you get started?

19. Which songs have vivid memories for you?

20. When was the last time you had to hold your tongue? What would you have said if you didn't have to?

21. What are 5-10 things that your parents don't know about you?

22. Make up an imaginary story about someone you see in your environment.

23. How do the opinions of others affect you?

24. I treat myself like…

25. Do you truly hate anyone? Who and why?

26. React to the following quote from *The Picture of Dorian Gray* by Oscar Wilde: "Every impulse that we strive to strangle broods in the mind and poisons us."

27. Write about a favorite memory of being recognized for something you did.

28. Write about a mistake that taught you something about yourself.

29. What is a reasonable way that you can adjust your morning routine to work better for you?

30. In what way is your biggest flaw also your superpower?

31. What do you know about the way your parents were raised? How did this influence their treatment of you?

32. In your mind, how do you imagine God or any higher power you might connect with?

33. What is a boundary that you need to draw in your life?

34. I got where I am today because…

35. How have you been able to gain the trust of others in the past? Write about a specific example.

36. How do you feel about humans traveling to, and possibly inhabiting, other planets?

37. How have you changed in the last year?

38. What is the quickest way to gain your trust?

39. Write a letter to your own body, thanking it for something amazing it has done.

40. What happens when you are angry?

41. What are five creative hobbies that you have never tried?

42. At what point in your life have you had the highest self-esteem?

43. What is a question that you are really scared to know the answer to?

44. Is there something that you could do a little bit less of to keep it from feeling like a chore or a burden?

45. What kind of worker are you? Are you satisfied with that?

46. If I could have it my way, everyone would just…

47. Write down 10 ambitious goals for the next decade.

48. What is a mistake you made in the past week. How can prevent it from happening again?

49. Which movies are your "comfort" movies? Any idea why?

50. If you could re-do a decade of your life, which would you re-do and why?

51. Write about an item from your past that you miss.

52. If you could eliminate any one disease or illness from the world, what would you choose and why?

53. Write about a dream that you can remember from the past. What does this dream mean to you now?

54. What is the hardest day you've ever gotten through? How did you get through it?

55. Scroll back through your camera roll and find the first picture that makes you smile. Write about the moment captured there and how it makes you feel.

56. What did you learn from your last relationship? If you haven't had one, what could you learn from a relationship that you've observed?

57. What is holding you back from being more productive at the moment? What can you do about that?

58. Who were your models of love and affection? What did you learn from them?

59. In your life, do you find that it works out better to plan ahead or go with the flow?

60. What life lessons, advice, or habits have you picked up from fiction books?

61. When is physical violence appropriate?

62. What are are some things you did with your dad/mom/other primary caregiver when you were young?

63. Use an online tool like the Random Classic Art Gallery to find a classic piece of art. Write about the thoughts or feelings generated by that piece.

64. Reflect on any meaningful family traditions you have. If you have none, which would you like to create?

65. Write a bit about physical pain and how it impacts your life and mood.

66. Invent your own planet. Draw a rough sketch of the planet and its inhabitants. How is it different than Earth?

67. Do you trust your intuition? Why or why not?

68. How has your self-worth changed over time?

69. What is a skill that you are proud of?

70. What are 3-5 memories that would help someone understand who you are as a person?

71. What are your strengths when working in a group with other people?

72. Do you think it's important to learn another language? Why or why not?

73. How could you be utilizing technology better?

74. Write a letter to your 9-year-old self.

75. Write about an aspect of your personality that you appreciate in other people as well.

76. React to the following quote from *We All Looked Up* by Tommy Wallach: "Do you think it is better to fail at something worthwhile, or to succeed at something meaningless?"

77. I have always survived by...

78. Describe your upbringing as you understand it today.

79. What was a seemingly inconsequential decision that made a big impact in your life?

80. List 5 things that you have enjoyed in the past. List 5 things that other people do that seem like they would be fun to try.

81. How would you like to be remembered?

82. I'm looking forward to...

83. What are your strongest sense memories?

84. Write about the last time you felt palpable heartache.

85. What is an experience you wish you could have again for the first time?

86. What is something that you grew out of that meant a lot to you at the time?

87. How did you bond with one of the best friends you've ever had?

88. Who was your first love? Reflect on the experience of falling in love for the first time.

89. Write about something that you would like to let go of.

90. Who do you feel like is treated unfairly in the world?

91. Which famous person (dead or alive) do you feel like you could be good friends with? How would you like to spend time with them?

92. What is an assumption people tend to make about you? How do you feel about that?

93. Who is somebody that you miss? Why?

94. What is a view about the world that has changed for you as you've gotten older?

95. Where in your body do you feel your anxiety? What is the first hint that anxiety is coming on?

96. Write 10-20 possible words to serve as a theme/goal for your year (my past two are "power" and "balance").

97. Who is on your team?

98. What does family mean to you?

99. If you've had a first kiss, write about what you remember. If not, how do you feel about that?

100. If you believe in an afterlife, what do you imagine it to be like? If not, how would you design the perfect afterlife?

101. If someone was narrating your life today, what would they be saying?

102. Write a letter to someone you miss dearly.

103. What are your favorite forms of self-care? How might you need to adjust your relationship to self-care at this point in your life?

104. How did your parents or caregivers try to influence or control your behavior when you were growing up?

105. How do you feel about asking for help?

106. Write a complete story with just six words. For example: Turns out the pain was temporary.

107. Observe your environment and try to notice 3-10 things that you've never noticed before. Write about them.

108. Write a letter to your 18-year-old self.

109. What unexpected event or disaster would you be totally unprepared for right now? Which would you be ready for?

110. Draw 25 circles on a page (5x5 grid of circles). Now set a timer for 3 minutes and try to turn each one into something unique. Could be a ball, hand cuffs, a logo, or an eye for instance.

111. React to the following quote from Elie Wiesel: "The opposite of love is not hate, it's indifference. The opposite of art is not ugliness, it's indifference. The opposite of faith is not heresy, it's indifference. And the opposite of life is not death, it's indifference."

112. What are some things that you could invest more money in to make life smoother and easier for yourself?

113. Are there any superheroes or other fictional heroes that you can't stand? Why?

114. Think about a "what if?" or worst-case scenario and work your way through the problem, identifying your options to get through it if it were to happen.

115. I deserve...

116. React to the following quote from Anaïs Nin: "We don't see things as they are, we see them as we are."

117. What is a fad that you totally fell into? How do you feel about it now?

118. Who do you consider to be courageous and why?

119. React to the following quote from Albert Einstein: "Life is like riding a bicycle. To keep your balance, you must keep moving."

120. Start by writing "why do I feel so _____?" Fill in that blank with whatever you are feeling today. Then try to work out the answer to that question.

121. What is the best thing you have ever written?

122. Listen to a song from a genre that you don't typically listen to. What thoughts, feelings, or other reactions are you getting?

123. Where in your life are you engaging in all-or-nothing thinking?

124. What would you like to be able to say "no" to more often?

125. Are there any conspiracy theories that you feel actually have some merit? Why or why not?

126. What physical or mental health issues in your family history do you need to watch out for?

127. Take a moment to close your eyes and listen to the sounds around you. What do you hear?

128. Make an old school collage out of magazine clippings, junk mail, or anything else you can find. See what themes or emotions are drawn out.

129. Write 3-5 things that you are proud of yourself for within the past week. Big or small.

130. Take a roadblock in your life right now and ask the question, "What would this look like if it were easy?"

131. What does "ready" feel like to you? How did you know you were ready for a major step that you have taken in your life?

132. Do something you haven't done since you were a child and reflect on the experience.

133. React to the following quote from *Inkspell* by Cornelia Funke: "Stories never really end...even if the books like to pretend they do. Stories always go on. They don't end on the last page, any more than they begin on the first page."

134. What piece of art has had the greatest impact on you? Why?

135. I wish I didn't have to go to...

136. Write about a time that you assumed the worst and things turned out better than expected.

137. Who have you genuinely helped in your life?

138. Who has been your greatest teacher?

139. What biases do you need to work on?

140. If you could choose between having a personal chef, a housekeeper, or a personal trainer for free, which would you choose and why?

141. What role does anger play in your life?

142. What are the 5 most beautiful things in your immediate environment?

143. Write about something (or someone) that is currently tempting you.

144. Do you believe the idea that you are the sum of the people you spend the most time with? Why or why not?

145. Where does your story really begin?

146. Find two unrelated objects near you and think of a clever way they might be used together.

147. What are five things you'd like to do before you die?

148. What are some positive things that you have taken away from the family culture in which you were raised?

149. In what ways are you currently self-sabotaging or holding yourself back?

150. It's been a while since I have…

151. React to the following quote from Martin Luther King Jr.: "Darkness cannot drive out darkness: only light can do that. Hate cannot drive out hate: only love can do that."

152. Write a letter to someone to whom you would like to apologize. Be as clear and unfiltered as possible. DO NOT send the letter.

153. What is your relationship to physical exercise? How might you need to change that?

154. What would be a "force multiplier" skill or habit that you could work on, which would make all the other things you are doing with your life just a bit easier?

155. React to the following quote from *Anterria* by Rebecca McKinsey: "One thing you have to realize from now on is that it doesn't matter if this is a dream or not. Survival depends on what you do, not what you think."

156. What are your attitudes and opinions about medication?

157. How do you take praise? How do you take criticism?

158. I learned a long time ago that…

159. What would you like your last meal to be?

160. What would be the best random act of kindness that someone could perform for you today?

161. What do you need to give yourself more credit for?

162. Talk about a time that you are proud to have told someone "no."

163. Write about 3 ways that anxiety has helped you in the past.

164. Who currently owes you an apology? What would you like them to say?

165. How do you feel when you spend time alone?

166. I've always felt too afraid to...

167. How does your internal self match (or not) your external presentation?

168. What role does jealousy play in your life?

169. React to the following quote from *The Art of Seeing* by Aldous Huxley: "Consciousness is only possible through change; change is only possible through movement."

170. What are you world-class at? Big or small. Important or unimportant.

171. When was the last time you felt let down? Think back on the experience and determine whether you feel the same way in retrospect.

172. How would you re-write the ending of a movie, show, fairy tale, etc. to make it more satisfying?

173. What's an indulgence that you haven't let yourself partake in recently?

174. If you had $500 to spend with no regrets, how would you use it to make your most perfect day?

175. Go somewhere that you can people-watch. Notice the different ways that people react to one another (or the ways they don't). Write some thoughts about what you notice.

176. Write about a big or small vacation you have taken.

177. How can you reframe one of your biggest regrets in life?

178. What do you wish more people knew about you?

179. What would a day in your life look like 10 years from now? Walk through it step-by-step.

180. When you were a child, how did you imagine your adult life? How does that compare to the way it is now?

181. Analyze a personal victory. Think of something that you did well and break down the active ingredients that allowed you to kick ass in that situation.

182. What is the most expensive thing you own? What is the story behind it?

183. What is a product that you wish you could convince people NOT to buy? Try writing an anti-ad for that product.

184. If you had more influence, what would you do with it?

185. What does death teach us about life?

186. In which areas of your life do you have the most control and which do you have the least?

187. Search "what can I make?" in Google and use one of the websites to figure out the recipes that you could make with the ingredients you already have on hand. Write 5 of them down and then try cooking one that you wouldn't have thought of. Write about the experience when you're done.

188. What has the role of shame been in your life?

189. What would be different about your life if you lived 100 years from now?

190. How would you like to change your relationship with your own body?

191. What would you do if you could stop time for two months?

192. Create your own conspiracy theory about a celebrity, public figure, monument, etc.

193. How do you feel when you see other people accomplish their goals?

194. Reflect on your attachment to your primary caregivers. If you have kids, compare that with their attachment to you.

195. What is the kindest thing someone has done for you?

196. What made you feel most alive when you were young?

197. Write a letter to your 13-year-old self.

198. Consider and reflect on what might be your "favorite failure."

199. Take a task that you've been dreading and break it up into the smallest possible steps.

200. What is your most meaningful possession? What is the story behind it?

201. What were the best and worst parts about your adolescence?

202. Write a letter to yourself 10 years from now.

203. What do you know about the start of your parents' relationship?

204. Do you believe that life has a purpose? Why or why not?

205. React to the following quote from Jim Butcher: "When everything goes to hell, the people who stand by you without flinching – they are your family."

206. React to the following quote from Emma Bull: "Coincidence is the word we use when we can't see the levers and pulleys."

207. The world would be a lot better if…

208. React to the following quote from Bob Marley: "The truth is, everyone is going to hurt you. You just got to find the ones worth suffering for."

209. Write about the weather outside right now. What does it make you feel like? Does it conjure up any memories? If you could do anything given the weather right now, what would it be?

210. Describe yourself in one sentence.

211. Do you feel like you gained anything from the books you were required to read in school? Why or why not?

212. What are some of your core values?

213. React to the following quote from Alice Walker: "The most common way people give up their power is by thinking they don't have any."

214. Imagine that you have arrived at a closed door. What does it look like and what's on the other side?

215. What would you consider to be your love language? What role does that play in your life?

216. I wish I never…

217. What is an assumption you have made about somebody else that turned out to be wrong?

218. What could you do to make your life more meaningful?

219. What images from your past (if any) make you feel safest? If none do, why not?

220. What keeps you going these days? Is that sustainable?

221. I wish someone would…

222. Try to write your full name with your non-dominant hand. Keep practicing until you fill up the page.

223. What sensations or experience do you tend to avoid in your life? Why?

224. What part of your work do you most enjoy? What part do you least enjoy? Why?

225. List 20 things that make you happy.

226. What are some small things that other people have done that really make your day?

227. How could you make something you dread just a little bit more fun?

228. Which quotes or pieces of advice do you have committed to memory? Why have those stuck with you?

229. How did/do your parents deal with adversity?

230. What situation is probably less risky or complicated than you are imagining?

231. Do you have any guilty pleasures? If so, why is it hard for you to own them?

232. What are your views on suicide?

233. React to the following quote from Steven Hawking: "We are just an advanced breed of monkeys on a minor planet of a very average star. But we can understand the Universe. That makes us something very special."

234. My life is nothing without my…

235. What pet peeves do you have? Any idea why they drive you so crazy?

236. Write a thank you note to someone. Sending is optional.

237. What do you wish you could do more quickly? What do you wish you could do more slowly?

238. Who is the most difficult person in your life and why?

239. How has your fashion sense changed over time? Would you like it to change more?

240. To me, love is…

241. What would things be like in 6 months if you continued your current trajectory?

242. What does the word "confidence" mean to you? What makes you feel confident?

243. What is something that you have a hard time being honest about, even to those you trust the most? Why?

244. What is your worst childhood memory? How do you feel thinking back on it?

245. What are some things that frustrate you? Can you find any values that explain why they bug you so much?

246. I can't believe that…

247. Are you taking enough risks in your life? Would you like to change your relationship to risk? If so, how?

248. Try giving yourself a topic to think about or problem to solve while you sleep. Be specific and write it down. Come back in the morning and free-write on the topic.

249. What were your parents' or caregivers' expectations of you growing up?

250. What is something that you feel a lot of people misunderstand about your family of origin?

251. How much do your current goals reflect your desires vs someone else's?

252. Why do you dress the way that you do?

253. Which emotions in others do you have a difficult time being around? Why?

254. What is your relationship with money and how has it changed over time?

255. Think of a cliché like "time heals all wounds" and argue for or against it.

256. How do you feel about the place that you grew up in? Would you change it?

257. What are some of the worst character traits that a person can have? When have you demonstrated these traits?

258. Write a letter to yourself 5 years ago.

259. You have been temporarily blinded by a bright light. When your vision clears, what do you see?

260. What would you change about your school experience if you had the ability to do so?

261. Name 5 smells that trigger happy memories for you and explain where they take you.

262. What is one thing you can change about today to make it more productive?

263. In what ways have you become more resilient over the years?

264. When I was younger I…

265. What can you do tonight to make sure that your body feels better tomorrow than it did today?

266. How could you be taking better care of yourself?

267. React to the following quote from *Into the Wild* by Jon Krakauer: "Happiness is only real when shared."

268. Do you feel like it's ever appropriate to be dishonest? Why or why not?

269. Do you feel like people understand you well? Why or why not?

270. How do you feel about the concept of nonmonagomous relationships (polyamorous, open relationship etc.)?

271. What can you recognize you are totally hypocritical about?

272. I wish my parents would have…

273. Pick something within 5 feet of where you are and draw it. Any style. Try to draw without judgment, even if you've never tried to draw before.

274. If you could live one other person's life, whose would it be and why?

275. Describe your favorite sound and what it means to you.

276. Try meditating for 10 minutes. If you already meditate, try meditating in a different way. Write about your experience.

277. What have you learned from previous jobs or involvements you've held?

278. Write the perfect guide that someone else could use to bring you comfort when you are feeling down.

279. Write a mantra that you can use today.

280. What plants and flowers do you feel most drawn to? What do they remind you of? How do they make you feel?

281. What is the most intense dream you can remember ever having?

282. What are your feelings and opinions about travel?

283. What is something that will seem barbaric 200 years from now?

284. If I were president, I would…

285. What are some of the self-fulfilling prophecies that have played out in your life?

286. What advice would you give to someone very much like you right now?

287. What is an opportunity that you are glad did not work out?

288. What small thing are you actually really proud of? Why does this mean so much to you?

289. Practice a call or conversation that you are avoiding. Write out both sides of the roleplay from start to finish.

290. Draw your life's timeline including the most relevant events that shaped you.

291. What are 5-10 of the most important aspects of your identity?

292. How do you feel about your city or town?

293. Where in your life are you taking things too personally?

294. Draw a "blind portrait" of someone or something around you. Use one continuous line without lifting your pen/pencil and don't look down at your page until you're done.

295. Who was your best friend from your youth? Do you still keep in touch? How has your relationship changed?

296. What kind of friend could you use right now?

297. If you could know one thing about the future, what would you want to know?

298. Close your eyes and imagine yourself somewhere safe. Describe the place that came to mind and reflect on what felt safe about it.

299. Who is someone in your life that you have always admired from afar, but never become close with? What do you admire about them?

300. What are a few things you could do to help you focus more when you need to?

301. What are the best and worst qualities you have inherited or learned from your parents/primary caregivers?

302. How do you know when it's time to let something (or someone) go?

303. What are the first things that typically come to your mind upon waking up. What do you make of that?

304. Try to write a short summary of the last thing you read.

305. Use the memories function or scroll back about a year on social media or your phone's camera roll. Reflect on what you see.

306. React to the following quote from Friedrich Nietzsche: "It is not a lack of love, but a lack of friendship that makes unhappy marriages."

307. Reflect on a time that you got into someone else's business when you should have kept to yourself.

308. Do something you do often, but in a different way. For instance, walk a completely different path than you normally do or drive to work silently rather than listening to music. Record your feelings and observations after.

309. Think of a negative assumption about yourself (ex: I can't make friends) and design an experiment to challenge that assumption.

310. Write a letter of support to someone that you care about. This can be someone you actually know or someone that you have never actually met. You don't need to send them the letter.

311. What is something that you have successfully grieved?

312. What would it look like if you planned for success?

313. Write about your happiest childhood memory.

314. Reflect on the nicest conversation you have had recently.

315. How has the past year changed you?

316. What are your top five comfort foods? What do they remind you of?

317. What are some simple tweaks that you can make to your environment to reduce anxiety?

318. Write about a recent experience that you loved being a part of.

319. What is an appointment that you can make for joy/pleasure/indulgence?

320. Who are you able to be vulnerable with? What makes them a person you are able to be yourself with?

321. Invent a holiday. How would you celebrate it each year?

322. What makes you feel most lonely?

323. What purchase under $100 has made the biggest impact in your life lately?

324. How would you like to die?

325. What is the title of your life story so far?

326. What is your relationship to debt? Are there any ways you would like this to change? If so, what's one step you can take in that direction?

327. What is a principle or ideal you'd like to pass down to the next generation?

328. If you could only keep three of your possessions, which would you pick and why?

329. What is a relationship that you need to improve in your life? What can you do to work toward improving it?

330. I wish I had…

331. Pick an item from your environment. Spend 2-5 minutes writing all the alternative ways you could use that item that do not include its intended use.

332. What is a belief that you are unwilling to change? What is one that you are still figuring out?

333. What are your feelings about the afterlife, ghosts, spirits, etc.?

334. How do you typically react when you realize you've made a mistake? Would you like to change that at all?

335. Write 10 words that you think are beautiful.

336. React to the following quote from Bill Watterson: "At school, new ideas are thrust at you every day. Out in the world, you'll have to find your inner motivation to seek for new ideas on your own."

337. Build a list of 10-15 songs that you can use to change your mood for the better.

338. What are some unique talents that you have?

339. React to the following quote from Tom Hiddleston: "Every villain is a hero in his own mind."

340. What organizations or structures do you think should no longer exist?

341. How do you feel about your job, current area of study, etc?

342. What is a chance that you have taken that paid off in the end?

343. When I think about the future, I...

344. What are your feelings about meditation?

345. Write 10 qualities that you appreciate in yourself (push yourself to get to 10) and 2 that you'd like to change or work on.

346. List 10 things that make you smile.

347. If you could ask one single yes or no question to the universe and get an answer, what would you ask?

348. What is something that you recently blamed yourself for? Now that some time has passed, how do you think about it differently?

349. If you were to give your anxiety a name, what would it be and why?

350. How do you feel about the age you currently are?

351. What is your first memory?

352. How did you like having fun as a kid? Has any of that carried over into adulthood?

353. Write about a favorite pet, past or present.

354. Which cultural mores, pleasantries, or standards do you find pointless?

355. What was the best part of the last year?

356. Assign a role (like peacekeeper, joker, or golden child) to each of your immediate family members.

357. What influences your attitudes toward sex and pleasure?

358. Are you satisfied with your sleep? If so, how did you achieve that? If not, what could you do to improve it?

359. If you could choose another career, vocation, or field of study than what you currently have, what would it be and why?

360. What fictional character do you most identify with and why?

361. What is a habit that you were successfully able to break?

362. If you could put anything you want on a billboard next to the busiest highway in the world, what would you put on it?

363. Make up a silly sport that doesn't already exist. What equipment is used? What are the rules?

364. What are some weird things you do when nobody else is around?

365. I hope that one day...

366. How could you improve upon the standard model human body?

367. What are some things that you judge others for that you would NEVER judge yourself for?

368. Right now I am... / I want to be...

369. What would the complete opposite of you look like?

370. React to the following quote from *The Invention of Hugo Cabret* by Brian Selznick: "I like to imagine that the world is one big machine. You know, machines never have any extra parts. They have the exact number and type of parts they need. So I figure if the entire world is a big machine, I have to be here for some reason. And that means you have to be here for some reason, too."

371. What are the top 3 emotions that you would like to embody today?

372. Describe the kind of person you are looking for right now.

373. Write a scene from your day in a poetic, descriptive way, as if it took place in a novel.

374. React to the following quote from *Man's Search for Meaning* by Viktor Frankl: "Everything can be taken from a man but one thing: the last of the human freedoms—to choose one's attitude in any given set of circumstances, to choose one's own way."

375. What activities make you enter a "flow" state and totally lose track of time? Could you integrate any of these into your life more?

376. React to the following quote from *The Alchemist* by Paulo Coelho: "No matter what he does, every person on earth plays a central role in the history of the world. And normally he doesn't know it."

377. React to the following quote from Lance Armstrong: "Pain is temporary. Quitting lasts forever."

378. What is the best thing you have ever created?

379. Stare in the mirror for two whole minutes. How did that make you feel?

380. Pull a random book from the closest shelf/pile and flip to a random page. Try to find a way that the words (or numbers or pictures) on the page apply to your life right now. No cheating.

381. What does normal mean to you? Is it good to be normal?

382. React to the following quote from *Coraline* by Neil Gaiman: "Fairy tales are more than true: not because they tell us that dragons exist, but because they tell us that dragons can be beaten."

383. What is a high and a low from your week so far?

384. What is your metric for success right now? What would you like to judge yourself based on?

385. React to the following: Many people forget that grief isn't only for people that have died. You also need to grieve lost experiences and expectations.

386. What do you feel like you have run out of time to do? Can you challenge that?

387. React to the following quote from *Stranger in a Strange Land* by Robert A Heinlein: "Love is that condition in which the happiness of another person is essential to your own."

388. Go outside and look at the clouds (or trees if you have no clouds today) and see what objects animals etc. jump out at you. Write each one down.

389. What is a memory that fills you with gratitude?

390. What freedoms are you most grateful for?

391. Which fictional world would you like to live in and why?

392. I wish I thought about _____ less often.

393. Aside from your own, whose voice do you hear in your head most often? What do they say?

394. What defense mechanisms kept you safe in the past, but may need to be let go now?

395. If you could design the perfect carnival or fair, what would be there?

396. In what ways do you need to change your physical health?

397. What was your last "light bulb moment" about?

398. What would someone learn about you if they could observe you for an entire day?

399. What is the best compliment that you have ever received?

400. If you had to go on stage and sing one song without making any mistakes, which would you pick? Prove it. Write all the lyrics to that song without looking them up.

401. What is the closest you've come to death? Reflect on that experience.

402. Realistically, what is the best way for you to have a positive impact on the world?

403. Which emotion is most difficult for you to experience and why?

404. If you aren't familiar with the idea of chakras, look them up. Do you feel like the idea has validity? How do you see them fitting into your life?

405. What is a cause that you are passionate about and why are you passionate about it?

406. What is something that moves you emotionally?

407. If I had more time I would...

408. If you could change one aspect of your romantic partner or best friend, what would you change and why?

409. Mentally walk through your day and identify ways you could change your environment to make things easier or smoother.

410. What are the major influences on your self-worth?

411. Make a doodle using only basic geometric shapes like lines, rectangles, circles, triangles etc.

412. Identify two random people in your environment and secretly wish for them to be happy. Say to yourself, "I wish for them to be happy." How did that feel?

413. Which words do you overuse the most?

414. How has your ability to entertain yourself changed since you were young?

415. What relatives have you felt closest to?

416. Write some lyrics to a favorite song and reflect on why they resonate with you so much.

417. If you could modify your living space to make it more pleasant or comfortable for you, what would you do?

418. Write about a time that your own strength surprised you.

419. Write a letter to your younger self when you were in a pivotal moment in your development.

420. Which animal embodies you and why?

421. If you had a million dollars, but could not use a single dollar on yourself, what would you do?

422. What can you not imagine living without?

423. What scares you the most? Why?

424. Reflect on your current relationship to social media. Do you feel like your social media habits (or lack thereof) are healthy?

425. Nobody knows that I...

426. When I think about my childhood, I feel...

427. What is something that you are insecure about? What is something that you are confident in?

428. What is a value of yours that you are not spending as much time as you would like on? What is something you don't value that you are spending TOO much time on?

429. If karma were real, what would you have coming your way?

430. What is the most important question to ask yourself every day?

431. React to the following quote from Tim Ferriss: "Being busy is most often used as a guise for avoiding the few critically important but uncomfortable actions."

432. Write a eulogy for a friend that is still alive.

433. When do you feel most comfortable in your own skin?

434. Are there any figures from history that most admire but you really don't like? Why?

435. How do you feel about the idea that one person should fulfill all the needs of their partner?

436. Reflect on something that used to be hard for you.

437. Write about a vehicle that can take you somewhere different from where you are now.

438. Write about something ordinary that made you smile in the past week.

439. What are some qualities that you admire in others? In what small ways can you integrate more of those into your life?

440. Why can't I just…

441. What is your relationship to spirituality? Has that changed over time?

442. What are your most common emotions these days? How do you feel about that?

443. What is something from your life that you still feel guilty for? What would help you feel more closure.

444. What do people get wrong about you?

445. What is a situation that caused you to confront your ethics?

446. What is currently your biggest time waster and what can you do about it?

447. Someday, I will…

448. If I could have one more chance, I would…

449. If you could talk to someone that you have lost for just five more minutes, what would you say?

450. What is your favorite weather or time of year and why?

451. What was your most embarrassing moment? Did you learn anything from it?

452. What would you do if you won the lottery?

453. If you could choose a superpower, which would you pick and why?

454. Who do you think of when you think of the word "successful" and why?

455. What does the word "courage" mean to you? How have you shown courage recently? How would you like to show courage?

456. React to the following quote from Maya Angelou: "I've learned that people will forget what you said, people will forget what you did, but people will never forget how you made them feel."

457. I find it very confusing that…

458. What standards do you apply to yourself that you would never apply to others?

459. If you could bring back one extinct animal, which would you bring back and why?

460. Write about something for which you would like to forgive yourself.

461. What are a few ways that you could use the evening to set yourself up for success the next day?

462. When I think about my future, I feel…

463. How do you feel about the concept of mental health diagnoses?

464. React to the following quote from *The Perks of Being a Wallflower* by Stephen Chbosky: "We accept the love we think we deserve."

465. What are some of the worst pieces of advice that you have gotten?

466. How could you add more fun or play into your life?

467. How could you better support your loved ones?

468. React to the following quote from Rumi: "If you are irritated by every rub, how will your mirror be polished?"

469. What is a necessary conversation that you are scared of having? Why?

470. How has your perspective on love changed over time?

471. If your life had been easier or harder, how would you be different now?

472. I wish I knew…

473. What are your main coping mechanisms right now? How are they serving you?

474. Build a list of 5 videos that you can watch when you need motivation.

475. Write about a near-miss in your life. Something that was almost perfect but ended up not working out. Could be a relationship, a job, or something else entirely.

476. Write three things that you have done well today.

477. I wish _____ knew that I _____

478. How do you tend to respond to crises? Write about your response to one that you can remember. How do you feel about that?

479. What age would you consider the prime of your life? If you haven't hit it yet, when do you think it will be?

480. Have you completely figured out your sexual orientation and gender identity? If so, reflect on that journey. If not, write about what you are still figuring out.

481. What is the most beautiful thing you have ever seen?

482. When do you most trust your instincts?

483. What motivates you right now?

484. What would make you feel more a part of your community?

485. Where will you be in 5 years if your physical health continues on its current trajectory?

486. If you won the lottery, who would you take care of and how?

487. What feelings do you have about your name? Were you named after anyone? Would you change your name if you could easily?

488. What is your relationship to crying?

489. What is something that you are avoiding right now? What makes it feel so insurmountable?

490. Are you satisfied with your sex life? Why or why not?

491. In what ways are you different than your parents or primary caregivers? How does that impact your relationship with them?

492. How would you like to feel in your body today?

493. React to the following quote from *The Kindly Ones* by Neil Gaiman: "Have you ever been in love? Horrible isn't it? It makes you so vulnerable. It opens your chest and it opens up your heart and it means that someone can get inside you and mess you up."

494. What memory makes you feel compassion for yourself?

495. Some say that animals are good judges of character. What do you make of that?

496. Who is the most charismatic person you can think of? What makes them that way?

497. Look up the lyrics to a song that you have never bothered to learn. Write down anything interesting that comes to mind.

498. What are your attitudes and opinions about therapy?

499. Consider a misfortune or roadblock in your life right now. Ask yourself, "What does this allow me to do?"

500. How do you feel about your country?

Printed in Great Britain
by Amazon

81050440R00031